Quentin Blake

LAUREATE'S PROGRESS

Quentin Blake

LAUREATE'S PROGRESS

JONATHAN CAPE
LONDON

For Michael and Clare,
and for Lois

LAUREATE'S PROGRESS
A JONATHAN CAPE BOOK 0 224 06481 9

Published in Great Britain by Jonathan Cape,
an imprint of Random House Children's Books

This edition published 2002

1 3 5 7 9 10 8 6 4 2

RANDOM HOUSE CHILDREN'S BOOKS
61-63 Uxbridge Rd, London W5 5SA
A division of The Random House Group Ltd.
RANDOM HOUSE AUSTRALIA (PTY) LTD
20 Alfred Street, Milsons Point, Sydney,
New South Wales 2061, Australia
RANDOM HOUSE NEW ZEALAND LTD
18 Poland Road, Glenfield, Auckland 10, New Zealand
RANDOM HOUSE (PTY) LTD
Endulini, 5A Jubilee Road, Parktown 2193, South Africa

THE RANDOM HOUSE GROUP Limited Reg. No. 954009
www.kidsatrandomhouse.co.uk

A CIP catalogue record for this book is available from the British Library.

Printed and bound in Singapore by Tien Wah Press [PTE] Ltd

Two precursors for Loveykins:

Frontispiece, The Owl in the
Pushchair (private collection).

This page, drawing for the
Chelsea Arts Club Yearbook.

Contents

Rough for Loveykins, *1999.*

Acknowledgements

This book is unlike *Quentin Blake Words and Pictures* in that the illustrations in it are chosen not from fifty years but from approximately three: the two years of the Children's Laureate appointment and the months immediately before and after. All the pictures in this book, with the exception of a very few, were produced during that period.

I would like to express my personal appreciation of the support of Waterstone's and the other sponsors of the Children's Laureate project, as well as of the generous collaboration of my publishers, the staff of the National Gallery and the Bury St Edmunds Art Gallery and those numerous other institutions who invited me as guest speaker or artist. Acknowledgements are also due to the many journalists who gave time and space and enthusiasm to describing what we were about. I am grateful too to those French teachers, librarians and booksellers who made me feel so much at home during the months of these two years which were spent in France. And not least to Lois Beeson, administrator of the Laureate scheme, and to my courageous assistants who never flinched as the correspondence rose around them.

The author and publishers would like to thank the following for their kind permission to reproduce material: RSA; Hutchinson for *The Red Shoes*; The Dyslexia Association and Egmont Children's Books; Fukuinkan-Fhoten Inc.; The Word; World Book Day and Macmillan Children's Books; the Polka Theatre, Wimbledon; The Year of the Artist; Action for Children's Arts; Junior Education; Book Trust; Home-Start; the National Campaign for the Arts; Faber and Faber for Ted Hughes' *Collected Plays for Children* and *Because a Fire Was in My Head*; Regent's Park Open Air Theatre; The *Daily Telegraph*; Jonathan Cape for *Loveykins*, *Roald Dahl's Revolting Recipes*, *Roald Dahl's Even More Revolting Recipes* and *A Sailing Boat in the Sky*; Red Fox for *The Laureate's Party*; the Department for Education and Skills; Egmont Children's Books for *More Muck and Magic*; Farrar Straus and Giroux for *Wizzil*; Rue du Monde for *Un Bateau dans le Ciel*; The British Library; Bury St Edmunds Art Gallery; The National Gallery; Enitharmon Press, the *Daily Telegraph* and the Arvon Foundation for *Mini Sagas*; The British Council; Bibliothèque de la Cité de Genève; Office du Livre de Poitou-Charentes; The Penguin Group (UK) for Savoury Crocodile and The Rough Guides to Children's Books; Woodmansterne Publications; The Royal College of Art; Brian Voce for the National Gallery photographs.

A page rough for Loveykins.

Phone Call

April 30th 1999. A telephone call from Lois Beeson, administrator of the Children's Laureate scheme. What she has to tell me is that of the three names on the shortlist for the first Children's Laureate the one that has been chosen is mine. This book is a sort of diary, log and scrapbook of the things that happen, the drawings that get drawn, over the two years of the Laureate tenure.

May 10th 1999. Morning in the National Theatre on the South Bank. Audience of writers, artists, publishers, children's book people; lots of children. The Children's Laureate is not, like the Poet Laureate, a royal appointment, but Princess Anne is there to start us off nonetheless. She hangs the gold and silver medal around my neck, and gives me the prize, a cheque for £10,000. (It isn't in an envelope. I tuck it into the top pocket of my jacket hoping I won't lose it.) I have to make a short speech, not more than five minutes. These are the words that I have written on a sheet of paper in front of me:

The Laureate's medal.

"Your Royal Highness, Minister, friends,

Erm. Generally when I have to say something in public I like to make it up as I go along, as more risky and exciting. But today, it matters and I want to try to get it right, so I have written something down. I am also considering that the five minutes I am allowed is really not very much in which to express the privilege I feel in being chosen for this honour. It is particularly valuable to me because I am aware that it is not only the response of the Laureate judges but that they also have the support of many others, including many schoolchildren.

"In thanking you for choosing me I don't want to get into that litany of thanks that is sometimes a feature of award presentations. Nevertheless I can't not mention the debt I owe to those authors whose words I have had the good fortune to illustrate and interpret – people such as

Russell Hoban, Joan Aiken, John Yeoman, Michael Rosen. (Where do you get your ideas from? Well, mostly I get them from authors. That's why I like them so much.) And I suppose I need hardly mention a similar debt which is to Roald Dahl. Many readers know me quite simply from my long collaboration with that extraordinary man, and I think I can say that without it I might very well not be standing here today. So that in a special way I also accept this award as a member of that team.

"I also feel privileged to be in the company of the two writers – I want to say "real writers" – on the shortlist. Their distinction gives me the measure of the value of this award. I am glad that I was not one of the judges who had to choose between three such different people, although being here, I have to say, feels more like collaboration than competition. I believe that is because people like us take writing children's books seriously, because we take writing

Illustration for
The Red Shoes.

Right, rough for
Mrs Armitage
Queen of the Road.

seriously; in the same way that those of us who draw take drawing seriously. And in that belief we can have surely no better support than the spirit and example of the poet who presides over this occasion today.

"Children's books, books for the young, are one of the most interesting and lively aspects of British publishing. We are amongst the world leaders. Even more to the point, however, is that these books, at their best, are primers in the development of the emotional, the moral, the imaginative life. And they can be a celebration of what it is like to be a human being. That is why they are important.

"One last thing. There is a letter to us from the Steering Committee of the award which says something like: 'You are supposed to do what you feel is appropriate; and you are meant to enjoy it.' I mean to enjoy it. I hope that we shall all enjoy it. Thank you."

Mrs Armitage got out to look at the damage.
"Hubcaps," she said.   "Who needs them?"
She took them off to the scrapheap, and
on they went.

Illustration for a book for the Dyslexia Association.

The Minister for Culture, Media and Sport, whose department has supplied the prize money, is there and gives an enthusiastic speech. There is also an energetic and personal one from Princess Anne, who subsequently ignores the programme written out for her and follows her own path, talking to everyone but mostly to the schoolchildren.

By the time I get home, my thoughts are already occupied with wondering about what things I'll be asked to do, what activities I'd like to propose, and how all that is going to fit into my timetable of work. Fortunately, one substantial task has recently been completed – a literary map of London for The Word, the London Book Festival. There is a book for each of the London boroughs, thirty-two in all – in the end it was only about eight days beforehand that I finally knew what they were all to be. It was like producing thirty-two miniature book jackets. No time to read all the books. Some I knew already; some I read very quickly or read part of, and for some

Swimming in my Dreams: illustration for a Japanese anthology, I Am Happy But I Do Not Know Why.

I just had to believe a synopsis. Sometimes I was lucky, as when I started reading Graham Greene's *The End of the Affair* and found the moment I needed, linking it to Clapham, in the first three pages.

Also recently, some drawings for *Beauty and the Beast* and for Hans Christian Andersen's *The Red Shoes*. (The Andersen was fascinating to illustrate although its morality is so dubious that it is hard to read it without a feeling of nausea.) These commissions are safely at an end; not so two picture books of my own. One is an odd story about a bird in a pushchair which is going to be called *Loveykins*. The other is about Mrs Armitage again, who has become Queen of the Road. When I did the first book about her I had no ambition that any other would follow, but the enthusiasm with which she seems to have been received (especially in schools, as a subject for writing and drawing) has encouraged me to produce a second and now a third

THE BUDDHA OF SUBURBIA
Hanif Kureishi

HENRY IV
William
Shakespeare

Colin MacInnes
ABSOLUTE
BEGINNERS

THE
CANTERBURY
TALES
Geoffrey Chaucer

THE SECRET
AGENT
Joseph Conrad

Muriel Spark
THE BALLAD
OF PECKHAM
RYE

Buchi Emecheta
ADAH'S
STORY

JACK MAGGS
Peter Carey

THE MAGIC TOYSHOP

Angela Carter

THE CARETAKER
Harold Pinter

Graham Greene

THE END OF
THE AFFAIR

Charles Dickens and, right, Samuel Johnson and
William Shakespeare for The Word *map of London.*

Left, cover illustration for The Children's Book of Books 2000.

Right, poster for the Polka Theatre.

adventure. It's unusual for me that both these books have got to the stage of having the words written and the roughs all drawn although no final drawings yet exist. My experience is that books of this kind need a lot of care and attention, and I rather suspect that they will have to be set to one side until there is a generous amount of time available for their completion.

May 11th 1999. Since the day before yesterday, the Laureate organisation has stopped being "them" and become "us"; so that I am able to say that this morning the newspapers have done well by us, in particular *The Times* and the *Independent* each with substantial articles under the headlines "HAIL TO MR MAGNOLIA" and "ONCE UPON A TIME THERE WAS NO BFG". They are particularly good at setting out the nature of the award, and explaining the way that it was brought into being through the collaboration of the children's book writer Michael Morpurgo and his neighbour in Devon, the late Poet Laureate Ted Hughes.

Happy 21st birthday Polka Theatre!

The award is for either a writer or an illustrator, and I have the advantage that I deal in both words and pictures (even though many of the words are not my own) so that both aspects are present from the start. I realise that in fact the relationship between the two is one of the things that I most want to talk about over the two years ahead.

May 20th 1999. Today is another interview, this time from one of the newspaper supplements. Long interview, apparently quite straightforward, but when the article finally appears it's apparent that the writer was either desperate for an angle, or just arrived with the notion that people who do children's books haven't grown up, symptoms of which she could find in the fact that I keep brushes in jugs and that the studio is untidy. It reinforces my sense that I am not wasting my time in emphasising that the skills employed in writing and drawing for young people are not in essence different from those you use in working for adults.

Illustration for poster advertising the regional activities of the Year of the Artist, June 2000–May 2001.

Above, logo for Action for Children's Arts.

Right, cover illustration for Junior Education.

Overleaf, poster-size illustration for
Junior Education.

May 28th 1999. Birmingham: first real encounter with the public, in this case a large audience of secondary school children, many of them from schools who had sent in reports on their own choices for Children's Laureate. Among the questions there is one about how many books I have illustrated, and I say that I have rather lost track of it but it must be getting on for two hundred. Girl's hand goes up in the audience.

   "You have illustrated two hundred and sixty-three books by eighty authors."

   "How did you know that?"

   "We counted them."

July 13th 1999. Interview with Anne Faundez of *Junior Education*. I'm pleased that she asks me to do two works for the magazine – a cover and a big picture which suggests a story for the spectator to imagine. Pleased because I've been worried, no doubt unnecessarily, that the

prospect of so much talking and writing might push drawing to the side.

November 4th 1999. I give the annual Patrick Hardy lecture for the Children's Book Circle. It's called "The Strange Story of the Unidentical Twins" and deals with the development and relationship of the verbal and the visual. I know this lecture will be published in the magazine *Signal*, but without much illustration, so I have decided to give a talk without any illustrations at all. Without visual ones, at any rate. I try to use examples from Shakespeare and Samuel Beckett to suggest that there are moments when the words have to do most of the work, and others (the ones the illustrator is looking for) where visual presentation can underline and expand the meaning. This, like many other talks, is one for adults, not children; people who are thinking about children's books.

Poster for National Children's Book Week.

Christmas cards for the charity Home-Start.

Drawing for Arts News, *the journal of the National Campaign for the Arts.*

Cover illustration for Ted Hughes' Collected Plays for Children.

November 13th 1999. The IBBY Conference (the International Board on Books for Young People). Today I can compensate by having lots of slides, lots of images. Impossible to do this talk without them, in fact, because I want to take the opportunity to explore the origins and influences of children's illustrators. I have the feeling that the history of the subject is studied perhaps too much within the history of children's books. Some of the best practitioners, like Cruikshank and Caldecott, came out of journalism, while there are influential artists – Rowlandson, for example – who never did anything specifically for children at all (though children must have seen what they did).

July 12th 2000. 9.30 a.m. Bousfield School Leavers' Assembly. It may seem rather strange, but one of the first decisions I made as Laureate was not to visit any schools – because to go to all that invited me would have been too exhausting, and to choose between them would have been invidious.

And talking to adults gets the message further faster. Bousfield has to be the exception. It's a junior school within five minutes walk of where I live, built on the site of the house where Beatrix Potter grew up, and a dozen years ago they invited me to come and give the prizes to the children who were leaving; they have invited me back every year since. This year is special because the final year pupils' dramatic presentation is based on my books. In the assembly we hear some of their memories of the school, and extracts from the show such as the "Improbable Records" song, and boys and girls in equal numbers in an imaginative modern dance version of *Clown*. Then I help give the books (everyone who is leaving has one) to Karim, Sebastian, Fjolla, Nikolina, Jihad, Ben, Mihaijlo, Mustapha, Zad and all the rest of them. By eleven o'clock I am on my way home and feeling ready for the next drawing and that the world would be better if it was a bit more like Bousfield.

PINOCCHIO
IN THE PARK
BY MICHAEL ROSEN

Directed by Emily Gray
Designed by Sophia Lovell Smith

May 12th 2001. A talk in the lecture theatre of the National Gallery for a family audience. I talk about my own work and the preparation of "Tell Me A Picture" (the exhibition described later in this book). I gave a very similar lecture in March, when all the 350 seats were sold and, as people were turned away then, I have been asked to do a repeat performance, once again to a full house. It falls happily a day or two before the announcement of the new Children's Laureate, and so it's my last official appearance. Between my first and this I think I must have done about thirty other talks from the Edinburgh Festival to the Oxford Union and the Royal Court Theatre. There has been also a clutch of television interviews and a number of broadcasts on radio, as well as newspaper and magazine interviews – maybe sixty items in all. I can't help remembering that before I knew it was to be me I had written to the organisers to say that I didn't think that the Laureate could be expected to give more than one important lecture, which could be published. There must be a moral here somewhere.

Left, poster for Regent's Park Open Air Theatre.

Above, illustration for an article in the Daily Telegraph *on children playing outdoors.*

May 23rd 2001. I can't resist adding one more appearance, though it properly falls after the end of the time. A police car collects me to take me to King's Cross Police Station, where I am to help launch a reading scheme organised for local children by Chief Inspector Dal Babu and his fellow officers. On the way I want to ask if we can have the siren, but haven't quite the courage to do so. Talk to the local reading scheme volunteers and teachers, and read the visiting classes a favourite story by Margaret Mahy, while at the same time drawing illustrations. Sometimes I have felt that the label Children's Laureate sounds antiquated or quaint, but it certainly does the business – the television people are on the scene and we make it onto the evening news. At the end of the morning the police car takes me on to my next appointment. The two young officers have the right idea about it. On arrival they both get out. One of them shakes me by the hand. "Good luck," he says, "and make sure you don't do it again."

Overhead projector drawings for talks in Edinburgh and at the Royal Court Theatre, London.

 Escalators

Although I set aside the two books I was working on at the time of the Laureate appointment I have still managed to get involved in nine others over the next two years. There's little point in giving diary dates when describing the development of a book; there is really only one serious date for an illustrator, the deadline, when the pictures have to be delivered. Work on one book also frequently overlaps with work on others, so that it's rather like looking at several versions of yourself going up parallel escalators moving at different, and irregular, speeds. Sometimes one starts later and arrives first. What is interesting to me about this batch is the diversity of them. Some represent types of book that I have worked on before, but the first escalator that starts moving is something completely new for me.

Random House (my main publishers, who publish this book) invite me to put together a list of my fifty favourite children's books. To begin with I think this is pretty straightforward, but quite

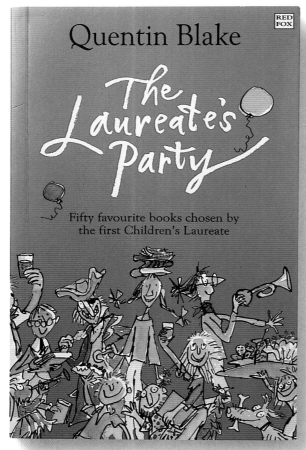

quickly I realise that I haven't read a children's book as a child for fifty years, and when I look at my first list I see that a lot of the books are either no longer available or for various reasons well past their sell-by date. Some survive, of course, but I have to start looking about for more recent favourites, including totally new ones. My list starts off with the youngest books – Beatrix Potter is the first – and ends up with one or two virtually adult books, such as *Great Expectations* and *The Member of the Wedding*. There's a lot more reading and re-reading than I had expected, but it also becomes more interesting than I had expected, too.

My idea is not to keep strictly to fifty but by various kinds of stratagem to drag in as many works as possible. I propose the title *The Laureate's Party* to suggest the welcoming nature of the exercise. It's a paperback but someone at the publishers has the idea of making the cover gold. A solid gold paperback!

While researching *The Laureate's Party* I also turn my thoughts to another book that I originally started some years ago. It's about my own illustration work, and I realise that this is the best time of any to complete it. One of the problems has always been that I am more interested in looking forward to the book I am going to do next than looking back at what already exists; but the Laureate scenario gives me the motivation that I need. My editor thinks of it as *The Art of …* but I say you can't write a book about your own work and call it that and eventually we settle on *Words and Pictures*. It deals with my own illustrations, not chronologically but in relation to various aspects of illustration – style of drawing, design of the pages, what you do about characters, and so on. Fortunately I already have a sort of skeleton of it in another, shorter book, *La Vie de la Page*, which I wrote for my French publishers in 1995 at the time of an exhibition in Paris. That gives me a flying start, which I need, and

which we all need, if the book is to come out in autumn 2000; which it does. The dust jacket gives me the opportunity to draw for myself a wild Laureate dressing-gown, the kind of thing I never wear in real life.

And then there is a quite unexpected invitation, this time from the DfEE, to produce some illustrations for a publication called *The Learning Journey*. It's the parent's guide to the Curriculum, which explains the thinking and intentions behind the teaching of the various school subjects, but also offers informal suggestions about ways in which parents can help their children's education. I am to provide illustrations to these last, and help to make attractive a document that might otherwise seem slightly indigestible. A whole series of vignettes of the everyday lives of parents, teachers and schoolchildren with suitable touches of exaggeration is right up my street.

This page and overleaf, illustrations for The Learning Journey, *the parent's guide to the Curriculum.*

Illustrations for More Muck and Magic.

Cover illustration for Because a Fire Was in My Head.

Two other books are linked by the coincidence that they are both anthologies, and both edited by Michael Morpurgo, initiator of the Laureate Scheme. Michael and his wife Clare have for the past twenty-five years run a wonderful charity called Farms for City Children. They have three farms and, though for all practical purposes the farms are like any other, to them, for a week at a time, come classes from inner-city schools – groups of children who otherwise would have no idea of country life. They're not there on holiday – they work on the farm. The results are extraordinary. In 1999, to help raise money for the charity, Michael edited a book of stories by contemporary writers called *Muck and Magic* and, following its success, the year 2000 saw a sequel, *More Muck and Magic*, for which he asked me to do both the cover and the illustrations. Michael Morpurgo's other anthology, *Because a Fire Was in My Head*, is of 101 poems "worth remembering". And certainly for me, also worth illustrating; not only because of the variety of subject matter and

Illustrations for Because a Fire Was in My Head.

Illustrations for Because a Fire Was in My Head.

Opposite page, illustration for Savoury Crocodile from Memories with Food at Gipsy House.

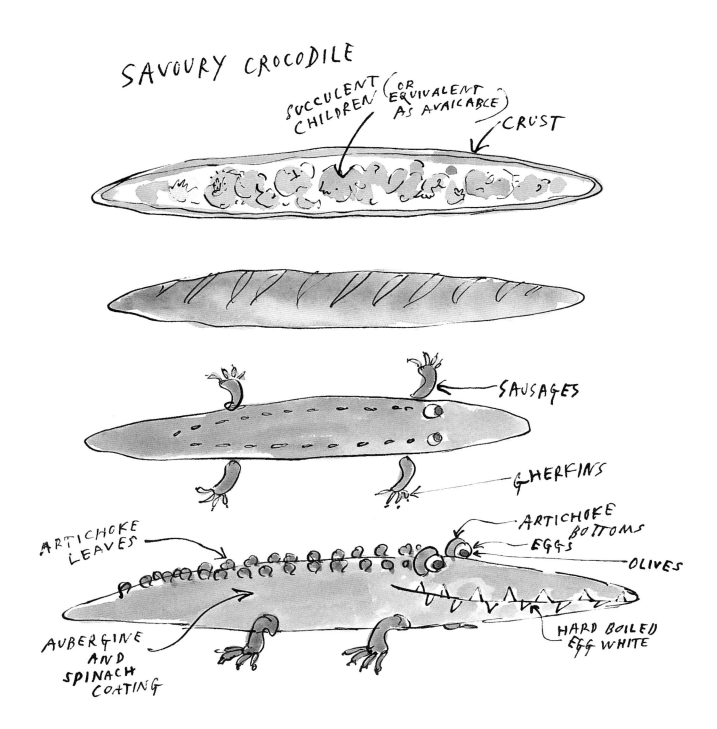

SAVOURY CROCODILE

SUCCULENT CHILDREN (OR EQUIVALENT AS AVAILABLE)

CRUST

SAUSAGES

GHERKINS

ARTICHOKE LEAVES

ARTICHOKE BOTTOMS

EGGS

OLIVES

HARD BOILED EGG WHITE

AUBERGINE AND SPINACH COATING

situation within these pages, but also the range of mood and emotion: from John Lennon to W. B. Yeats; from Lewis Carroll to John Masefield; from *Timothy Winters* to *The Rime of the Ancient Mariner*.

The next book involves a quite different approach: it's *Roald Dahl's Even More Revolting Recipes*. Dahl, as his myriad readers know, had a specially strong line in food; sometimes delicious (pheasant for dinner), sometimes bizarre (all those sweets in *The Giraffe and the Pelly and Me*), and, of course, sometimes disgusting (the Twits' wormy spaghetti). And Dahl's home, Gipsy House in Buckinghamshire, is somewhere there has always been a lot of good cooking and eating and drinking, so that the first ever Dahl cookery book was a straightforward one — a collection of recipes gathered from family and friends by Roald and his wife, Liccy — *Memories with Food at Gipsy House*.

My contribution to that was a recipe for Enormous Crocodile; the special ingredient was the

Scrambled Dregs

This page, rough, photograph and finished illustration for Scrambled Dregs, Roald Dahl's Revolting Recipes.

Opposite page, rough, photograph and finished illustration for suckable pencils, Roald Dahl's Revolting Recipes.

cocktail sausages, which were supposed to represent portions of the succulent infants that he had recently consumed. (Of course, in the book he never does consume them, but that was not going to deter me.) My idea was that it was a dish that conceivably you could prepare, and could eat – but it was a visual joke, really, and I never expected anyone to do so. However, somebody did. Nothing daunts Liccy Dahl's kitchen collaborators, and it was not long before, to my surprise, I saw before me a three-dimensional, edible crocodile – and one that looked far more like the real live thing than my first diagrammatic representation.

I would be happy to think that this was perhaps the first step in the direction of all the subsequent Revolting Recipes. At any rate some years later Liccy, having set up the charity The Roald Dahl Foundation in memory of her husband, had the idea of producing a book to publicise and raise funds for it. This was *Roald Dahl's Revolting Recipes* and I was asked to help illustrate it. I say "help" because

there were also stunning photos of the food by Jan Baldwin, and the tricky part was to bring the drawing and the photos happily together. First of all each of the dishes had to be cooked experimentally, and then tested, and then there were Polaroid photos taken of each of them. Once I knew what Mudburgers or Lickable Wallpaper or Frobscottle looked like I could do a rough drawing showing how they might appear on the page, and then, with the guidance of those roughs, final photos were taken with, say, the plate at the correct angle or the glass appropriately tilted. After that I could do my final drawings, each accompanied by an overlay to show where the photo should appear when everything was put together by the designers and the printers. Another sort of cookery, if you like.

Now, five years later, we set about *Even More Revolting Recipes*, because the pages of Dahl still contain so many tantalising edibles – Grobswitchy Cake, Boiled Slobbages, Lizards' Tails.

Illustration for The Royal Breakfast from Roald Dahl's Even More Revolting Recipes.

We know the routine now so that we can set about it all more speedily although, once again, there are delicate moments, such as getting the angle of a plate of soil with engine oil just right.

The next escalator starts off with a call from Holly McGhee in New York. She is the agent for William Steig, who has written a new book called *Wizzil*. Will I illustrate it? This is an extraordinary request in several ways. One of them is because when I first looked at copies of the *New Yorker* as a schoolboy fifty years ago, there were already cartoons by William Steig in them – probably drawings of those tough little kids he called "Small Fry". Later on, Steig developed in those pages drawings of a more poetical fantasy, before bringing his wonderfully idiosyncratic vision to the world of children's books. And he is a great illustrator – why should he want me to do it? I think perhaps I discern an answer: at the age of ninety, is he feeling a little tired?

But no, it isn't that – he is just too busy with other projects. Another curiosity about *Wizzil* is that it takes place in rural America – not in the imaginary world of no particular time and space where William Steig easily finds himself at home (think of *Shrek*, for instance). Wizzil, though she is a witch, lives in real enough surroundings.

It means that I have to summon up whatever resources of memory and reference I can find; after all, I have looked at many American paintings, photographs and movies, and I have illustrated *Huckleberry Finn* and *Sarah Plain and Tall*; and in any case I am not going to miss the opportunity of drawing Wizzil turning into a fly and walking down the face of DeWitt Frimp, or of collaborating with a twentieth-century graphic hero. He sends me one or two encouraging faxes, and I forge ahead. William Steig, thank you for *Wizzil*.

The other picture story book of these two years has a more complicated genesis. Twenty-five

years ago or more I was first published in France, and Gallimard Jeunesse have been my main publishers there ever since (though not the only ones). My editor then, Christine Baker, is still my editor now. Partly as a result of this French connection I bought myself a house in the southwest of France, where I spend several months each year.

So that one day a librarian in the nearby Rochefort library, Marie-Hélène Monteagudo, notices that she has an illustrator of children's books in the region, and tracks me down. The next spring, by arrangement, I set aside a day to visit the library. No ordinary library, incidentally. The ancient ropeworks of Rochefort – La Corderie Royale – is a seventeenth-century stone building three hundred and sixty-five metres long. Recently restored after the dilapidations of the 1939–45 war, it has at its centre generous library spaces for both adult and young readers. It is here I turn up expecting to sign some books and perhaps draw a picture or two; but that is not what they

Illustrations for Wizzil.

have in mind. First of all there is a visit to two classes. One has with the help of their teacher written a story incorporating characters from a number of my books and they have also invented a sort of canapé, bearing something to eat for each of the characters – honey for the bear, a fly for the frog and so on. The other class has written a continuation of *Mrs Armitage on Wheels* (she is called Armeline in France), ready for my instant illustration. And then there is lunch. This is a meal, prepared by a handful of stalwart ladies in large aprons, which comes entirely from *Revolting Recipes*, with menus written out in wobbly handwriting by the children. After lunch we draw a large dragon on a roll of paper on the library floor, and after that is the *pièce de théâtre*. Mrs Armitage once again, but now on an exercise bicycle on a movable stage, pushed by two small boys wearing waistcoats announcing the Armeline Fan Club. Actors and audience go from the motor-hooter stall to the place

where you buy umbrellas and so on along the banks of the Charente.

The following year there is a sun-filled June evening when, on a temporary stage, thirty Clowns are put through their paces by children not much bigger than they are; Daisy Artichoke meets the Enormous Crocodile, to his moral improvement; and a class of children appropriately dressed as dogs and cats and rats and plumbers' apprentices actually erect the do-it-yourself House that Jack Built.

It is on such an occasion that I find myself talking to a group of local teachers. They have organised themselves into a group called LSA 17, which studies children's picture story books (which the French call *albums*), both for their verbal and visual qualities and for their possible uses in the classroom. Geneviève Roy is their leader, and she explains to me that this year they want to extend their activities by a collaboration with an author/illustrator. The idea is that that person is

Performance in the grounds of the Bibliothèque de la Corderie Royale.
Clockwise from far left, Cockatoos, the Enormous Crocodile, the House
that Jack Built and thirty Clowns.

going to create a book – a real book, and one, they hope, that will eventually be published – based on the suggestions of classes in schools in the region. Nobody mentions who that person is, but there is no other author/illustrator present; and though I am not sure if the question has actually been asked, it is there in the room between us all right; will I be that person? I am conscious that it is slightly mad to take on anything else at this moment and I am also aware that the idea is attractive and in addition I am touched that they are asking a foreign visitor to join them. How can I say no? I don't.

But what is this book to be about? It is to be *"sur l'humanisme"*; not, as I first imagine, about humanism, but about humanitarian issues – bullying, racism, pollution, war. How to start off such a project for all the children who are to be my collaborators? Normally I cast about tentatively for some basic image, situation, fable – but this time I can't delay. I need both a boy

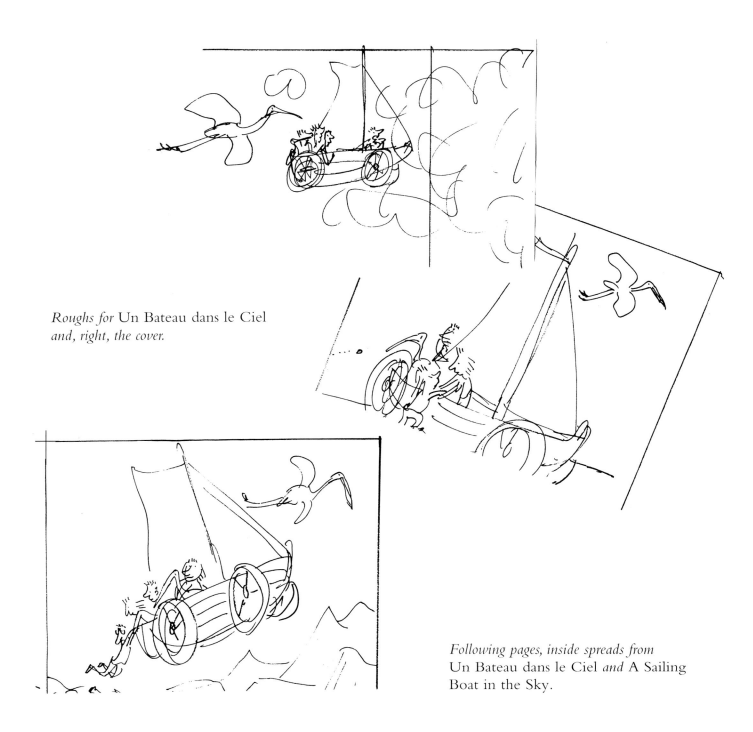

Roughs for Un Bateau dans le Ciel *and, right, the cover.*

Following pages, inside spreads from Un Bateau dans le Ciel *and* A Sailing Boat in the Sky.

and a girl, but I also need some way in which they can encounter a scenario of distress. As we are near the sea I decide I can put them in a boat; and when I come to do a handful of rough drawings I give it the utmost versatility I can imagine – a boat that can go on the sea or on the land, and even fly. The teachers select three of these drawings, take them into their classrooms and begin to explore their possibilities. When the results of their discussions and writings come back it becomes clear that almost everyone has gone for the opportunity to fly.

And so we pursue the story. Via the Internet we can involve other French-speaking schools, in London, Dublin, Sweden, Luxembourg – even in Singapore. The amount of material for our local teachers to organise and select from becomes enormous; but select from it they do, and from their selection I put together a rough version of the whole book, using as many of the children's ideas as can be made to fit together. It goes back to the schools for further work – more ideas, sug-

Quentin Blake

Un Bateau dans le Ciel

R U E D U M O N D E

gestions for dialogue. To push it along we have two big meetings, one in La Rochelle and one in Rochefort, each of several hundred children, where I do my best to egg them on, and they in their turn sing songs, perform sketches, read poems – the work in school has not been restricted to the story itself but has also created many side-whirlpools of interest.

From the children's writings I stitch together a text, and the time has come when we need a publisher. Normally, of course, my publisher in France is Gallimard; but following their advice I approach a small publishing house, quickly becoming better known, called Rue du Monde, which specialises in books about contemporary issues such as ecology and children's rights. It is run by one man, Alain Serres, who initially responds with an appropriate element of caution – a book by children, as he points out, isn't necessarily a book for children. But this, we agree, is a book by me, even though one in which I have 1,800 collaborators. Once we establish that, the road (do I

Inside spreads from Un Bateau dans le Ciel.

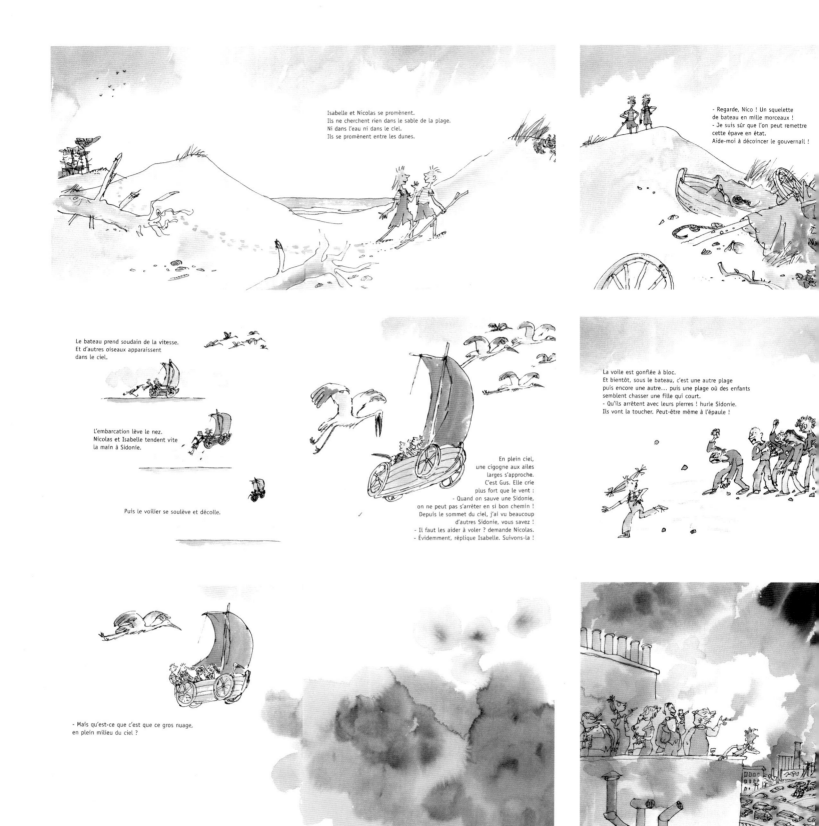

Isabelle et Nicolas se promènent.
Ils ne cherchent rien dans le sable de la plage.
Ni dans l'eau ni dans le ciel.
Ils se promènent entre les dunes.

- Regarde, Nico ! Un squelette
de bateau en mille morceaux !
- Je suis sûr que l'on peut remettre
cette épave en état.
Aide-moi à décoincer le gouvernail !

Le bateau prend soudain de la vitesse.
Et d'autres oiseaux apparaissent
dans le ciel.

L'embarcation lève le nez.
Nicolas et Isabelle tendent vite
la main à Sidonie.

Puis le voilier se soulève et décolle.

En plein ciel,
une cigogne aux ailes
larges s'approche.
C'est Gus. Elle crie
plus fort que le vent :
- Quand on sauve une Sidonie,
on ne peut pas s'arrêter en si bon chemin !
Depuis le sommet du ciel, j'ai vu beaucoup
d'autres Sidonie, vous savez !
- Il faut les aider à voler ? demande Nicolas.
- Évidemment, réplique Isabelle. Suivons-la !

La voile est gonflée à bloc.
Et bientôt, sous le bateau, c'est une autre plage
puis encore une autre... puis une plage où des enfants
semblent chasser une fille qui court.
- Qu'ils arrêtent avec leurs pierres ! hurle Sidonie.
Ils vont la toucher. Peut-être même à l'épaule !

- Mais qu'est-ce que c'est que ce gros nuage,
en plein milieu du ciel ?

- Cette poulie, c'est pour ce bout de bois et la roue, c'est...
- Je trouve ce bateau de plus en plus bizarre, mon pauvre Nicolas !

Sur les dunes, le vent venu de la mer commence à souffler.
La vieille voile se gonfle.
Et voilà l'étrange bateau qui se met peu à peu à rouler sur la plage.
Isabelle et Nicolas semblent glisser sur le sable.
- Un inconnu à bâbord ! lance Isabelle.

- Je suis Sidonie, une cigogne blessée.
Juste là, à l'épaule. Un coup de fusil
qui m'interdit de voler.

- Monte vite ! lance Isabelle. Le bois de notre bateau
est plus solide que leurs cailloux.
L'enfant s'accroche. La coque du bateau protège la fillette.
Elle s'appelle Éloïse.

Sous le ciel immense, la Terre est immense.
Là-bas, loin de tout, Isabelle et Nicolas
aperçoivent des hommes forts qui travaillent.
À côté d'eux, des enfants minuscules
sans force et sans âge.

Ils travaillent aussi.
L'un d'eux ne parvient même plus
à soulever sa pioche.

Le bateau frôle le sol.
Isabelle, Nicolas et Éloïse attrapent
le garçon épuisé, du bout des doigts.
- Tu sais, explique Éloïse en lui épongeant le front,
la voile de notre bateau est plus douce que le vent.
Sidonie approuve et prête ses plumes au front de Rachid.

- Regardez !
Nous sommes
au-dessus d'une ville
gigantesque où tout fume :
les habitants, les maisons,
les usines, les voitures...

Éloïse s'interrompt et se met à tousser.
Rachid et Nicolas se mettent à tousser en se pinçant les narines.
Sidonie se met à tousser en claquant du bec.
Et Isabelle se met en colère :
- Mais vous ne voyez pas ce garçon
qui n'en peut plus de respirer la fumée ?

- C'est à mon tour d'agir,
lance Gus en plongeant.

The boy was called Eric, and he was so happy
to be able to breathe again. They all felt much better
as they sailed peacefully through the bright clear sky.

'But what's that noise?' said Nicholas.
'Is it some kind of storm?'

There were holes in the boat, the sails were torn
and there were so many people on board
that it was sinking lower and lower in the sky.
'We must find somewhere to land soon,' said Nicholas.
'But where?'

At last they came to another beach.
'How about there?' suggested Gus.
'We can't land there,' said Nicholas. 'Look at that
awful woman with the green face. Do you
think she's a witch?'

They all busied themselves taking the boat to pieces.
Upside down the hull made a shelter
where Magda and Lira could rest.
Isobel and Eric hung the sails up
to make a hammock.

Nicholas turned one set of wheels into a sort of washing line,
and Simona and Gus used the other for a nest.

Rachid collected wood for the fire,
and Eloise helped her granny
with the cooking.

The fish soup that night was very good. Eloise's granny had
added a few special ingredients, including a flying fish
to help Simona's wing get better quickly.
'It would be lovely if you could all stay here with me a bit longer,' she said.
'Yes, but how can we?' said Nicholas. 'We've got our parents.'
'And friends,' added Rachid, 'a long way from here.'
'And a lot of journeys still to make,' said Gus.
It was at that moment that Rachid noticed a ruined cabin
at the end of the beach.

Inside spreads from A Sailing Boat in the Sky.

It wasn't a storm.

It was warplanes, rockets and deafening explosions. They were in a war zone. 'We've got to get out of here!' cried Isobel. 'But wait!' she said. 'We must try to save that woman and her baby.'

The woman told them that her name was Magda and that her baby was called Lira. All hands were needed to help them safely aboard.

But they were not safe yet . . .

'Don't be silly,' said Eloise. 'There's nothing to be afraid of. She's my granny and she sells fish on the beach. Everybody thinks she's lovely.'

Look, with all those planks we could build another boat – a much, much, bigger one!' 'And I know what,' said Eloise's granny. 'I can stitch together all my old dresses, my curtains and my handkerchiefs, and you'll have the most beautiful sails in the world!'

And so one bright morning, when Simona was able to fly again, there was an amazing new sailing boat in the sky.

And what happened after that, you will just have to imagine . . .

Quentin Blake à Rochefort

Poster illustration for an exhibition in Rochefort.

mean the sky?) is open to us. Fortunately Alain Serres is a writer and poet as well as a publisher, so that he immediately gives us a title for the book (*Un Bateau dans le Ciel*) and reworks the text so that it becomes easy and fluent and ready to appear in the world alongside other books by professional writers. For me there remains the major task of completing the forty pages of finished drawings. I have to say "major task" not only because of quantity but also because, although when I first said yes to the project I had envisaged it as something that might be carried out in a fairly swift and detached fashion, by this stage I have become so involved that nothing will do but a focus as intense as I can manage. In June, in France, I get the pictures finished; by September, brilliantly, Alain Serres produces the final book. Everything has happened within the space of a school year.

It has been, as one of the teachers described it, *une belle aventure*; and, I now realise, almost like another version of a Laureate life, in parallel, and in French.

Drawings on the Wall

March 2000. An exhibition at the British Library, showing off some of their most interesting books and manuscripts and called "Chapter and Verse". Each section of the exhibition is marked by a large model book, perhaps ten feet in height. Each book is of a different plain colour, but the library has invited me to illustrate the cover of the book which introduces the section devoted to children's books – in a sense to produce a giant book jacket. The drawing itself is done at manageable size on my drawing desk, and then enlarged and coloured and stuck on the book. It is going to be a useful technique in future.

February 2000. First meeting of the patrons of the Campaign for Drawing. The campaign has been started by Julian Spalding, Master of the Guild of St George. The charity with that curious name was established over a hundred years ago by John Ruskin, with the broad aim to improve the world. Julian Spalding's idea is to mark the centenary of Ruskin's death by a three-year project

CHI
BO

Illustration for Chapter and Verse *at the British Library.*

THE BIG DRAW

The Campaign for Drawing: logo for The Big Draw.

Opposite, award certificate and Drawing Power logo.

Come and draw

to emphasise the importance of drawing for both adults and children – an activity that Ruskin engaged in with great skill almost every day of his life.

To me, a patron is someone whose name appears amongst others on the writing paper of a charity or other organisation to show that it has friends and supporters; who turns up once in a while but is not expected to do much. I discover that the Campaign for Drawing – perhaps because it is small – does not work like that. You have to roll up your sleeves. I offer to draw a logo for the campaign, and then one for a national day of drawing, called "The Big Draw". As we discuss it I suggest that you can't have something called "The Big Draw" without doing a Big Drawing. Someone else suggests that we should do it in a tunnel – the one that leads from South Kensington Underground Station towards the South Kensington museums.

September 2000. We're in the tunnel. Lined with lavatory tiles, not very well lit, and about a

quarter of a mile long, it isn't the most attractive of places. But there is a lot of paper already up on the walls, thanks to London Transport, and free artist's materials, thanks to Crayola, and teams of helpers from the museums identified by special T-shirts, and no lack of artists, not to mention droves of passers-by. The Natural History Museum team has brought its own skulls and bones by way of inspiration. Perhaps the best moment for me is when I'm taking a stroll along to see how everything is going and I'm accosted by one of the helpers: "Have you thought of doing any drawing today?" Some areas of paper become simply accumulative, like a large telephone pad, but it is also noticeable that individual finished drawings are respected. An hour from the end, and the whole place is full of drawings and people drawing and has developed the benevolent air of an extremely long studio filled with artists happily at work.

The purpose of this initial drawing effort is essentially to bring attention to the real "Big

Illustration for an article on drawing in the Guardian.

Opposite, poster for A Baker's Dozen.

Draw" when, on a Saturday three weeks later, three hundred museums and galleries across the British Isles invite the general public in to take part in a wide variety of drawing activities. The Campaign for Drawing subsequently gives a number of award certificates to the most striking and inspirational of these, and my experience of being a patron is extended still further. Would I give out these certificates? Agree to that. Perhaps twenty-four hours later: would I also *draw* the certificates?

August 23rd 1999. The Bury St Edmunds Art Gallery in Suffolk invites me to help curate an exhibition of children's book illustrators. Irene Edwards is the education officer of the gallery, and already has clear ideas about the sort of show she wants it to be – first, not only an exhibition of originals, but also of preliminary work, roughs and sketches, which will introduce the spectator to the various approaches and ways of thinking of each artist. I like this, because it matches my wish to emphasise the skill and experience that go into drawing and writing for children.

An exhibition of contemporary children's illustrators co-curated by Quentin Blake

A BAKER'S DOZEN

chosen by Quentin Blake

Angela Barrett
Alison Bartlett
Stephen Biesty
Patrick Benson
Quentin Blake
Emma Chichester Clark
Sara Fanelli
Martin Handford
Satoshi Kitamura
Neal Layton
Nick Manning &
Brita Granstrom
Chris Riddell
Charlotte Voake

Bury St Edmunds
ART
Gallery

St Edmundsbury
BOROUGH COUNCIL

a touring exhibition organised by Bury St Edmunds Art Gallery   east england arts

Illustration by Quentin Blake 1999 © the artist

Second, the artists will all be young or youngish – some well established, but still with the shine on reputations established over the last decade or so; others with just one or two books to their credit. There are twelve of them, and the show will be called "A Baker's Dozen"; I am along as the thirteenth – some kind of ink-stained old-timer who has been here before.

August 26th 1999. Meeting at the National Gallery in London. On my behalf Lois Beeson has put forward to two or three major museums and galleries an idea for an exhibition combining both illustration and paintings. The most positive reaction is from the National Gallery and their education department. To my pleasure and amazement, we get an almost immediate response to say that the Bernard and Mary Sunley Room is available from February to June 2001 and that we are in business.

September 1999. At the National Gallery again so that we can compare our thoughts about the exhibition. My basic idea is that illustrations, recent paintings and Old Master paintings will hang together in alphabetical order, so that there is no hierarchy of respect or importance. In addition there will be no titles or information on show apart from the name of the artist, so that the emphasis is placed on the spontaneous uninhibited reactions from the spectator. Michael Wilson, the National Gallery's director of exhibitions, is sure that there should only be one artist, one work, for each letter of the alphabet. I enquire how I fit into this; and is it a choice under "B" between me and Botticelli? He explains that he doesn't see me as one of the exhibiting artists; however, the walls of the National Gallery are large – what about drawing on them between the framed works?

"Are you allowed to do that?"

Some unusually quiet moments in
The Sunley Room at the National Gallery
during the Tell Me A Picture *exhibition.*

"We want it to be as little like the National Gallery as possible."

And off we go. I am helped and guided by Ghislaine Kenyon, the deputy head of education, and together we select the pictures. It proves to be more complicated than I had envisaged, but our ideas about education match up well, and there are no vexing committees and compromises. We get contemporary children's book illustrations from several countries: Innocenti, Jozef Wilkon, Zwerger, as well as modern works by Hopper, David Jones, Paula Rego, Ken Kiff. For me there are also discoveries among the Old Masters, because although I am familiar with the paintings we choose by Uccello and Piero di Cosimo, I have walked through the collection in the past without noticing small mysterious paintings by de Nomé and Elsheimer, or an engaging picture of a Parisian street theatre by an artist I don't know, Gabriel de Saint-Aubin.

May 8th 2000. For a few days the Sunley Room is empty between exhibitions, and we can get a sense of what it is like to be in it. I make rough sketches so that I can estimate the scale of the drawings on the walls. We decide to hang the pictures lower than usual to make them closer to the young spectators. Later on we discover that for adults (at any rate for those of 5 foot 7 inches in height) there is also a sense of a more intimate possession of the works.

October 2nd 2000. An exhibition at Chris Beetles' gallery in Ryder Street to launch *Words and Pictures.* Somehow or other I have managed to put together two hundred and twenty-five pieces of work – roughs, layouts, second versions, third versions, one-offs – which seems to me rather a lot; but Beetles is a believer in quantities of everything on these occasions: champagne, food, crazy music – and sales, of course.

This page and overleaf, wall drawings for Tell Me A Picture.

O

Emily Mary
Osborn

Wall illustration also used as a poster for Tell Me A Picture.

Illustrations from the book
accompanying the Tell Me A
Picture exhibition.

February 14th 2001. "Tell Me A Picture" opens to the public. It's half term and there are queues up the stairs inside the National Gallery. The wardens are slightly alarmed by so many young fingers so near the works that they are there to protect, but the mood is friendly and people are talking to each other. I rather suspect the wardens get to enjoy it too.

The room is able to accommodate four visiting classes each day in sequence, and before the show opens it is already fully booked for the four months of its run. Over that time there are a quarter of a million visitors, about twice the expected average. I am relieved to discover that the drawings on the wall (which are not really drawn on the wall but enlarged onto vinyl and stuck on) don't act as a distraction. As Ghislaine Kenyon writes later, "This cheerfully familiar, near life-size crew had the effect of halting the children in their instinctive rush to get to the end of anything; being children, they understood the game, you looked at the drawings and then moved

Poster for Tell Me A Picture.

Advent calendar for the National Gallery, 2001.

National Gallery, LONDON

2001

Illustration from the Tell Me A Picture *exhibition book.*

on to look at what the drawings were looking at with such engagement."

The book of the exhibition is also called *Tell Me A Picture*. It isn't a simple catalogue. In it, as in the exhibition, you see each work of art on its own without comment, alone on a double-page spread. On the intervening pages more children make random comments and enquiries; except, of course, they are not random, but quite carefully reflect some of the questions you would want raised in (say) the classroom. The exhibition also has a website where you can view each picture and offer your own suggestions for its title and story. The four thousand visits it receives come from adults as well as children – in Spanish, Italian, Finnish, Dutch and other languages, as well as in English, and from as far afield as South America and Australia.

June 17th 2001. Last day of "Tell Me A Picture". Unfortunately I am not there to see it, though I am happy to remember that on a previous occasion one visitor said to me, "We think it ought to go on for ever."

Ex-Laureate

May 17th 2001. I invite a lot of friends to celebrate the end of my tenure at something I call the Ex-Laureate's Party. The invitation itself has a drawing of me (or the badly-shaven alter ego who stands in for me in Laureate drawings) delivered to the dustbin. But nothing quite as final as that happens; there are evidently still things for an ex-Laureate to go on doing, and it is perhaps the moment to abandon the eternal present-tense of the diary mode in favour of something like an epilogue.

Looking back from the day on which these words were delivered to the publishers I can see a number of Laureate streams trickling on. Further involvement, for instance, in "Young at Art", that imaginative project that the London Institute, which directs London's art schools, runs with secondary schools. It was at one of their exhibitions that I encountered Diane Henry Lepart, who invited me to become an active patron of her scheme for a National Youth Gallery of Art and Design; a gallery which will – we all hope – present adult work in ways that will speak to a young

Bookplates downloaded from the Internet for
The Home Library Scheme *initiated by Anne*
Fine, the second Children's Laureate.

audience, as well as show young people's own work; a gallery which will effectively belong to them.

One Laureate-like activity has both preceded the Laureate years and gone on after them. This is my participation in the festival of children's books each November at the French Institute, which is truly Franco-Britannique and brings books and writers together in their own languages and in translation. In 2001 the French illustrator Bruno Heitz and I performed drawings of each other's national stereotypes – perhaps the most amiable duel imaginable.

A completely new venture was one proposed by the British Council: an exhibition of present-day children's book illustration. My co-curator was Andrea Rose, arts officer of the Council; we called the show "Magic Pencil". Designed eventually to travel, it was to start life at the Laing Art Gallery in Newcastle, where it would be able to salute the newly established Centre for the Children's Book, before coming to the British Library. At the same time my exhibition at Rochefort library saw a

Drawings for Mini-Sagas, the Arvon Foundation compilation of 50-word stories.

Illustration for the cover of Magic Pencil, *the catalogue of the* British Council *exhibition of children's book illustrators of today.*

new lease of life as part of a series of activities in southwest France which annually pursues the aim of introducing adults to children's books, and I was able to put together a second exhibition of originals for the Bibliothèque de la Cité in Geneva.

There was one other occurrence that produced a strange sense of disorientation or enjoyable dizziness, when two or three of my friends suggested that I might like to use my archive of drawings as the basis of some kind of gallery with my name on it. I have nearly all the originals of my book illustrations as well as many other drawings – there must be two or three thousand of them – and it would be wonderful if this were a way of giving them a continued active life. Though a majority of them are from children's books, I would hope such a gallery would be about not simply my books or children's books, but the art of illustration in all its forms. It could provide a home for exhibitions of young illustrators, foreign illustrators, illustrators from the past, and

Quentin Blake
Illustrateur

Bibliothèque de la Cité
de Genève

Place des Trois-Perdrix – 1204 Genève
Exposition du 5 mars au 27 avril 2002

GALLIMARD JEUNESSE

Poster for a French conference to introduce adults to children's books.

Cover illustrations for the two volumes of The Rough Guide to Children's Books.

Two Christmas cards for 2002 specially drawn for the Quentin Blake series of greetings cards, published by Woodmansterne.

open a lot of other portfolios and archives that we rarely or never see.

Amongst these dreams and happenings there was one that, to me at least, was of no less significance. Though the precise date escaped record, at last the finished drawings of *Loveykins* were completed and delivered. And with that creature safely on the wing, I can now get *Mrs Armitage, Queen of the Road*, onto the road. I can also look forward to future drawings. All I know at the moment of writing is that I have started some, and that I seem unable to keep birds out of them. Embarking on a set of pictures to submit for the Summer Show of the Royal Academy, whose members have recently elected me an honorary fellow, I find myself drawing pictures of women drawing birds. They are either stuffed birds, or very well behaved: they make small, dark, angular marks that contrast with the human figures. Although the technique is a different one, they hark back to drawings I used to do many years ago in the aftermath of days spent in the Chelsea Art School

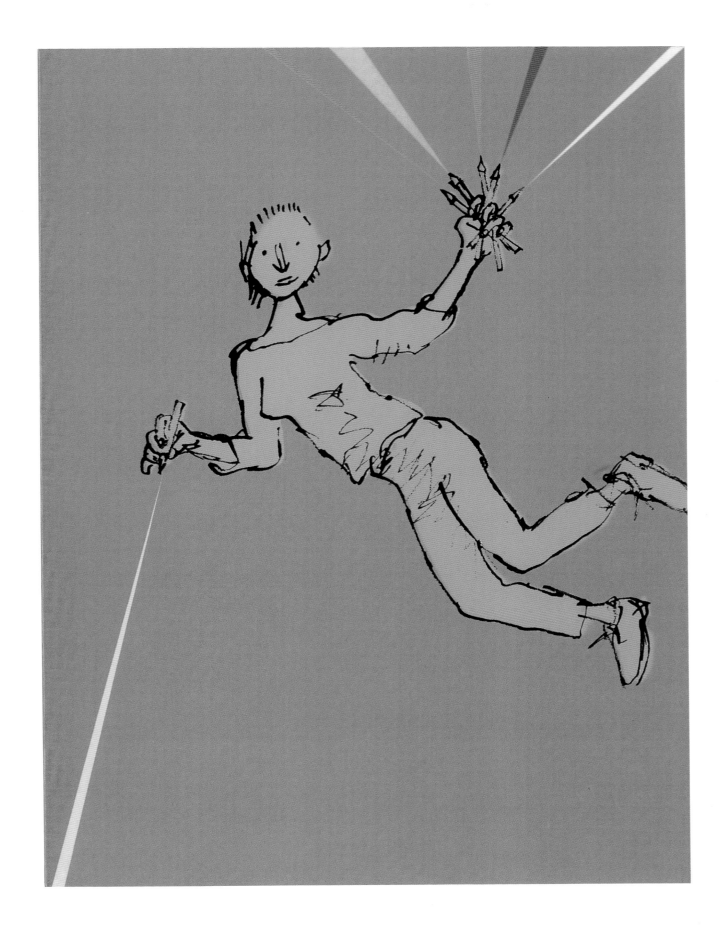

'Angel of Art and Design' Christmas card for the Royal College of Art, 2001.
Drawn with a reed pen on Arches paper, processed using Adobe Photoshop at the College.

'My goodness,' said Angela. 'It's a baby bird
blown out of his nest. He needs someone to look
after him.'

Pages from the book Loveykins, *2002.*

She wrapped him up carefully in her scarf,
and off home they went.

*Drawings of people as birds, 2002. The Young Poet
and, right, The Old Reader and the Young Reader.*

life-room; like them, for better or worse, they are invented, not observed.

Another sequence of drawings which I began tentatively in the hope that it might one day make an exhibition is of people *as* birds. Nothing unusual about that, essentially – it's an old and much-frequented tradition, and one that has often included four-legged creatures as well. However, I think it is the fact that birds are two-legged, like us, that gives them something of our balance and gesture and makes them nearer to us. Birds-as-people is also a way of talking about people, and somehow I find it enables me to draw characters – down-and-outs, businessmen, fashionable mothers – that I wouldn't attempt otherwise. I go at them with a black watercolour pencil, which is a new implement for me, and the necessary reminiscence and information seem to seep in from somewhere. The second stage is to brush water, or watercolour, into the drawing, when it bleeds black copiously and you really have to pay attention if you want to bring it through.

And what else? When I deliver this manuscript to my publisher he will ask what my next book is to be and, though I have at the moment no idea, I think we shall part in an optimistic spirit. I hope, too, that I may soon be surprised by some unexpected manuscript. I hope that the next project will have some new aspect to it, even though it is apparent that it is drawn by me; and that perhaps, in some indirect way, these two years of Laureate drawing and talking and writing may colour and contribute to the result.

Whether they do or not, I wouldn't have missed them for anything.